Contents

About Making Charts

You can often find out as much from pictures as from reading words. Some **information** is easier to understand in a picture.

Some facts can be shown clearly in a picture or chart.

Imagine you've looked into a rock pool on the beach. You might have found these sea creatures:

You might start by putting them in groups. This helps you to see more clearly what you've found.

This is called **sorting** or **classifying** objects.

Then you could count each group and make a chart like this one.

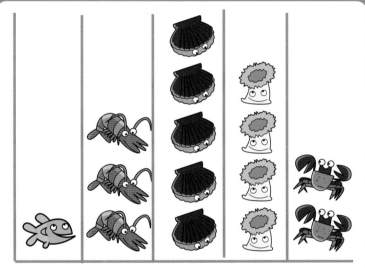

The chart is divided into bars, or columns. The size of the columns shows how many things you found.

Which is the tallest column? This shows that you found mostly shellfish.

This book shows you how to make and understand charts like this. They are called **pictograms**.

Finding out

To make your own pictogram you'll need to find out some information. There are lots of ways to do this. You can ask people, or count things or measure them.

What's your favourite ice-cream?

Information from other people

Sometimes you will get your information from other people. You could ask them questions or ask them to **vote** for a favourite of some kind.

Information from things

Lots of information comes from counting things.

You might count how many people in your class have dark hair, how many have fair hair and how many have red hair.

Colour of hair in our class

Brown hair //////

Red hair //

Fair hair /////

Black hair ///

Weather at lunchtime

Monday = sunny

Tuesday = rainy

Wednesday = sunny

Thursday = cloudy

Friday = cloudy

You could record the weather at lunchtime for a week and list the days it rained, the days it was cloudy and the days it was sunny.

Asking questions

When you make a chart, you might get your information from other people.

You could ask people to put their hand up if a dog is their favourite pet, or a cat, and so on. You would need to count the hands each time.

Making a survey

You could do a **survey** instead. This is useful if the people you want to ask aren't in the same place at the same time. You write down your questions and ask people one at a time to give their answers.

Work out the best way to ask your question.

If you just ask people which animal is the scariest, you might get too many different answers to make a pictogram.

Which animal are you most scared of?
tiger /// crab,
tiger, lion,
scorpion, bee //
hippo
shark fierce dog wolf
snake shark //
wasp
slug

It's best to give people some answers to choose from. Then you know all the answers will fit your pictogram.

sharks

Which of these is the scariest animal?

shark ////
tiger //
lion ///
spider ////
wasp /

Investigate

Another way to **investigate** is to do an experiment and **record** the results, or take measurements.

Fruit
apples //////
bananas //
grapes /////
pears ///
oranges //

You could look at the type of fruit in everyone's lunchbox and write down which fruit people have brought to school.

Less is more!

Don't try to get too much information. A small number of choices is easier to record.

If you take measurements, make sure you always measure things in the same way so that you make a fair comparison.

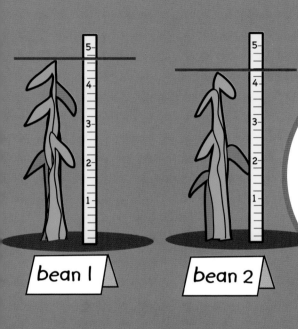

bean 1

bean 2

When you record a measurement, use the nearest whole number.

height of beans
week 6

bean 1 = 5 cm

bean 2 = 4 cm

Enough!

Small numbers of things will make your chart easier for others to read.

11

Check it!

It's a good idea to check that you are getting your information in the best way. Some ways are better than others!

At the gate

Suppose you wanted to find out how children come to school. One way is to stand at the gate counting people as they arrive.

How children get to school

car ///////////////////

bus /////////////////////

on bike ///////////////////////

on foot /////////////////

The hard way

It's hard to count the number of children in cars and buses, because lots of children may arrive at the same time.

A better way

It's better to go around the classes and ask how many people come to school by each type of transport.

class 2
30 children
car –/////////
bus –/////////
on bike –/////
on foot –/////

Final check

- Count the number of people in the survey and the number of ticks. Are they the same?
- Did you measure or count the right things?
- Did you ask the right questions?

Lines and piles

A pictogram shows a picture of each thing in a column or bar. It's not the same as making a line or a pile in real life.

Make a line

Ask everyone to bring their coats in from the cloakroom. Sort the coats by colour and put them in separate lines – red coats, blue ones and so on.

Count how many coats there are in each line. Some coats are bigger than others, so the most common coat colour may not make the longest line.

Pile them up

Now make piles of coats. Put each line of coloured coats into a separate pile.

Your piles are not like a pictogram. You can't tell from the height of the piles which is the most common colour.

Some coats may not fit your piles easily. You might need to start a new pile.

Neat and tidy

A pictogram would use the same size of picture for each coat. You could tell how many there are of each colour from the heights of the bars.

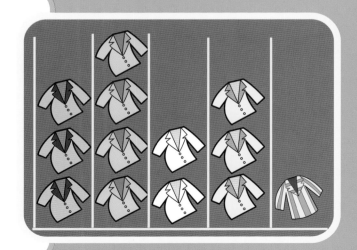

Looking good

To help people understand your chart it should be easy to read, and the pictures you use must suit your information.

Using icons

Your teacher will help you pick pictures that show what your chart is about. Pictures used like this are called **icons**.

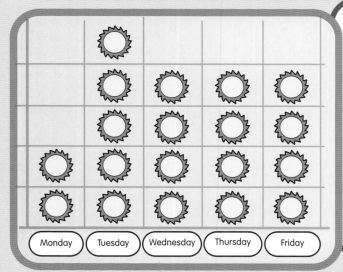

| Monday | Tuesday | Wednesday | Thursday | Friday |

You might use the same icon in each bar. If you had counted the hours of sunshine each day for a week, you might put suns in each bar.

The icons might be completely different. If your chart shows the fruit people have in their lunchboxes, you might use a different fruit picture in each bar.

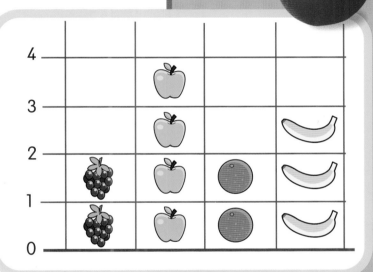

How many icons?

Look at the information you have gathered for your chart. Does it need just one icon or lots of different icons? If it needs lots, which ones?

Start a chart

It's time to practise putting information into a chart on the computer.

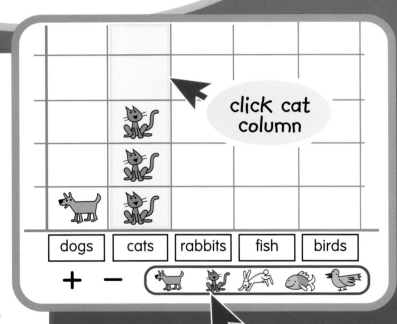

click cat column

then click cat four times to enter 4 cats

Getting started

You may be able to choose how many columns to have on your pictogram.

You may be able to give a name, or label, to each column.

Type the numbers or click a button for each number. If you wanted to enter '4' for the cats column, click on the cat picture four times.

Get it right!

If you make a mistake, put it right. When you've finished, check the numbers again by looking at the information you found out.

Pets in our class

dogs 2

cats 4

rabbits 3

fish 4

birds 1

- Have you copied all the numbers correctly?

- Have you missed any numbers out?

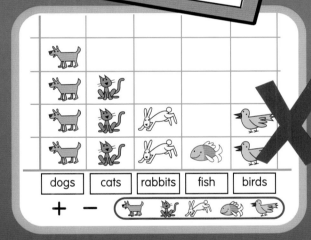

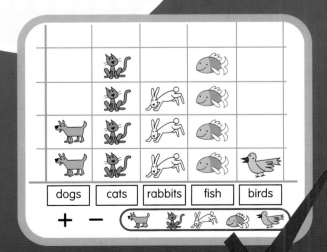

Making sense

You know what the chart is about – but other people need to be able to read it, too.

Use a title

You'll need a title that explains what the chart shows. Make it short but clear.

Year 1 lunchboxes

How we get to school

How many in my family

Favourite fish

Numbers

Putting numbers up the side of the chart helps people see how many things there are in each column without having to count them.

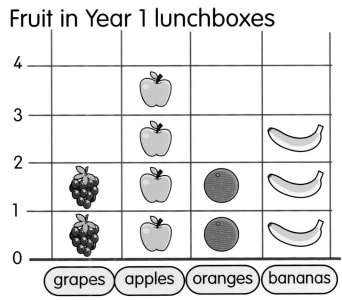

Fruit in Year 1 lunchboxes

Anything else?

You can put the date on your chart if it will help people to understand it. If it is a weather chart, it matters whether it was in summer or winter. Four sunny days in a row would be more surprising in the winter than in the summer!

What does it mean?

Looking at a pictogram can tell you a lot of information.

How many?

You can see from the height of each bar how many things are in each group.

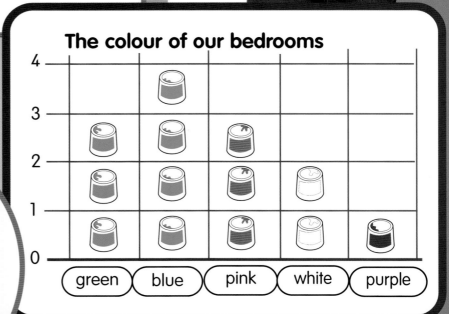

The colour of our bedrooms

You can see how many children have each colour in their bedroom. How many people have pink bedrooms?

Picking favourites

Compare the size of the bars. The tallest bar shows you which is the most common colour.

The most common colour of bedroom is blue. Pink and green are the second most common colours.

The least common colour is purple – only one person has a purple bedroom.

Comparing

The bar for blue bedrooms is twice as tall as the bar for white bedrooms. This tells you that twice as many people have blue bedrooms as white bedrooms.

What doesn't it mean?

It's good to know what a chart shows you – but it's important to remember there are some things it doesn't show you.

Take care!

In the chart, more people have blue bedrooms than any other colour – but that doesn't mean most people have blue bedrooms.

Of the **13** bedrooms in the chart only four are blue – that's less than half!

You can't say that blue is the children's favourite colour for bedrooms.

They might not have been allowed to choose the colour. Or they might share a bedroom with a brother or sister and had to agree on a colour they both quite like.

You can't tell...

You can't tell from the chart which child has which colour.

You can't tell whether more girls than boys have pink bedrooms.

You can't tell whether older children all have blue bedrooms.

You can't tell if shared bedrooms are more likely to be painted white.

Over to you

Now it's time to make a pictogram of your own.

Which sport do you like best?

What pets do you have?

Choosing a subject

Decide what your pictogram will show. Here are some ideas, but you could choose something totally different:

- What sorts of pets people have.

- Favourite sports.

- Types of trees – in your garden, at school or in the park.

Getting information

Work out exactly what information you need. Remember to ask your question in the same way every time. Make sure people understand the question and the type of answer you need.

Don't choose a subject that will be too difficult to investigate.

- If you are counting things or people, make sure your numbers are right.

- If you look at how people come to school, are you going to count people or types of transport?

- If you look at fruit in lunchboxes, don't count each grape separately!

Making your chart

Put your information into the computer. Check that you've put it in properly and correct any mistakes. Choose icons that show what your pictogram is about, and add labels.

What have you found out?

What can you tell from your chart? Which is the top sport? Do children prefer apples or oranges for lunch?

What don't you know?

What sort of information can't you tell from your chart? Is the information you've got the most useful? Or might people want to know different facts?

Check your work

Think about how you've made your chart.

• Would different icons have been better?

• Could you have used clearer labels?

• Did you ask enough people?

• Can you make the chart any better?

Glossary

Classify	Put objects into groups.
Icon	Small picture that stands for something.
Information	Facts about something.
Investigate	Find out about something.
Pictogram	Chart that shows how many things there are of different sorts by showing pictures in a column, or bar.
Record	Write down information.
Sort	Put objects into groups.
Survey	Ask people questions and write down their answers.
Vote	Show which you prefer or choose a favourite.

Index

Making Charts
and the National Curriculum

The work in this book will help children to cover the following parts of the National Curriculum ICT scheme of work: unit 1e, part of unit 1c. It can be tied in with work on science and maths.

Make sure the pictogram software is set up ready for the children to use. They will need suitable icons to be available. You will need to choose suitable text fonts and sizes.

Encourage children to work together and discuss options as they collect information and make their pictograms. Ask them to state what they are trying to find out. This will make it possible to assess how successful they were. Review their finished work and ask them to talk about why they chose the options they did, and why they rejected others. Ask them if they can think of any ways of improving their work.

Children should be encouraged to review, evaluate and improve their own work at all stages. If possible, show them work by older children and help them to see how this fulfils the same aims that they have in their own work.

Contents

Words printed in **bold letters like these**
are explained in the Glossary.

Who uses Orthodox churches?

Orthodox Christians brought their religion to Britain and elsewhere when they left their own countries to escape wars or other problems. These Christians wanted to **worship** in the way they had always done.

At home Orthodox families pray in front of pictures, called **icons**. On Sundays and times like **Christmas** and **Easter**, they also worship in special buildings called churches.

This map shows some countries from which Orthodox Christians came to Britain.

Britain
Russia
Ukraine
Serbia
Greece
Cyprus

An Orthodox family prays at their icon corner.

Where are they?

Orthodox churches are usually found in large towns and cities. Many are in buildings which once belonged to another Christian group. Some have been specially designed for Orthodox worship.

Some Orthodox churches have a **community centre** beside them. Here people born locally learn about their religion and the customs of the countries it came from.

This church in Coventry, England, was built for Greek Orthodox Christians.

What do they look like?

The outside of an **Orthodox** church may be very plain, with only a **cross** to tell you it is a church. It may also have a small belfry (bell tower) and a **dome** in the centre of the roof.

Most Orthodox churches are simple outside, so that the inside will look even more beautiful.

A Serbian Orthodox church in Birmingham, England.

Going inside

When Orthodox **worshippers** go into their church, they use gestures to show their devotion to **God**.

They make the **sign of the cross**, take a candle and walk respectfully up to a desk. On it is an **icon**. This **holy** picture shows the person or story that **Christians** remember at that time of year. The worshippers kiss the icon, then light their candles, placing them in a stand. The candle flame shines like their love for God.

Worshippers kiss the icon when they first enter the church.

What will I see first?

In **Orthodox** churches **icons** usually cover the walls and the ceiling. These icons are arranged to tell the story of **Jesus** and his **disciples**, linking them with other famous people from the **Bible**.

The most beautiful icons cover the **iconostasis**. This is a screen with doors in it. It divides the main part of the church from the **sanctuary**. In the sanctuary is a special table called the **altar**, and other things used in **worship**.

Looking towards the iconostasis.

Icons

Icons teach the Orthodox belief that **Jesus** is the Son of **God**. In the **dome** of many churches there is an icon of Jesus, shown as **Christ**, Lord of the Universe. Above the sanctuary there is usually an icon of Mary, his mother. Other icons are of the **saints**, people who once lived close to God and are

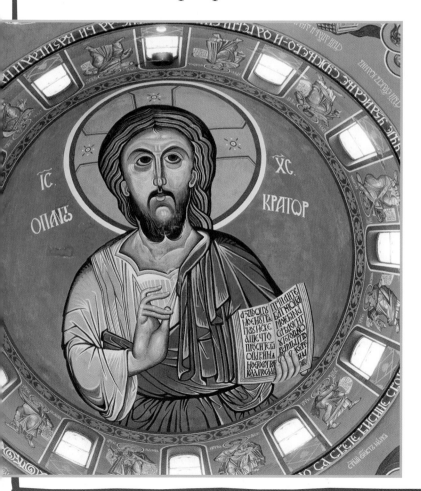

now believed to be worshipping God in **heaven**.

The glowing colours of these icons help people feel closer to God. For the worshippers the icons are windows into heaven.

Icon of Christ in a dome.

What else is there?

There will be some seats, often only a few around the walls. This is because people usually stand during **services**.

There is a place for the **choir**, usually near the **sanctuary**. In **Orthodox** churches the human voice is the only instrument used in **worship**, so you don't see any musical instruments. Services are sung from start to finish.

You should also be able to see a throne for the **bishop** when he visits the church. A bishop is an important church leader.

A bishop's throne.

In the sanctuary

On the **altar**, in the centre of the sanctuary, you will see the book of the **Gospels**. The Gospels are four important books in the **Bible**, the **Christian holy** book.

On a side table there is usually a special plate and cup used in **communion**. Beside them is the **incense** burner and the **banners** used in **processions**.

All of these things are richly decorated. The best things people can afford are used in worshipping **God**.

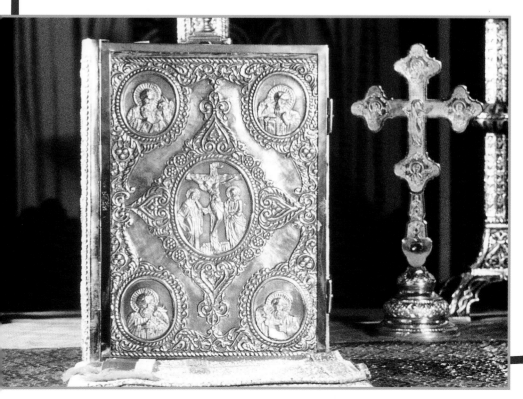

The book of the Gospels on the altar.

Who will I meet?

If you visit a church on a weekday you may see those who take care of the building and the **priest** who is in charge of the **worship**.

In the evenings and at weekends you may also meet the **deacon**, who helps the priest, and singers who come to train the **choir**. Teachers and youth club leaders come to work with groups in the **community centre** next to the church.

Lessons in the community centre.

Name days

If it is somebody's **name day** the priest may meet a family in church. On name days he **blesses** the special bread which they bring to church. He may join them at home in a celebration meal.

The priest blesses a name day loaf.

Name days

Each **Orthodox** boy and girl has a name linked with a **saint** or a **Christian** festival. As well as their birthdays, children also celebrate the day on which their saint is remembered in the church.

Name day ceremonies are not the same in every Orthodox church.

What happens on Sundays?

Many **Christians** come to church on Sundays to celebrate **Jesus's resurrection**. This is the day Christians believe **God** brought Jesus to life again, after his death on the **cross**.

This important service is called the **liturgy**. It begins at about ten or eleven o'clock and lasts up to three hours. During the liturgy **worshippers** usually stand facing the **iconostasis**. Sometimes men stand on the right and women on the left.

Worshippers facing the iconostasis.

The liturgy

During the liturgy the **priest** is helped by two or more **altar boys**. All are dressed in special robes. These show that they are leading worshippers into God's presence.

The book of the **Gospels** is carried from the **sanctuary** with lights and **incense**. This shows that Jesus's life and teaching are like a light to the world.

The priest reads part of the Gospels and explains the meaning of the reading.

The priest reading part of the Gospels with altar boys beside him.

Holy Communion

Later in the **liturgy** the **priest** carries a plate and cup in **procession** round the church. These hold bread and wine and are covered with special cloths.

The bread and wine remind **worshippers** of Jesus's last meal with his **disciples** and his death on the **cross**. The disciples were Jesus's closest followers.

Everyone bows their head as the bread and wine are carried round the church.

16

Tasting

The plate and cup are placed on the **altar**. The priest prays that **God** will use this bread and wine to enter the lives of those who take **communion**.

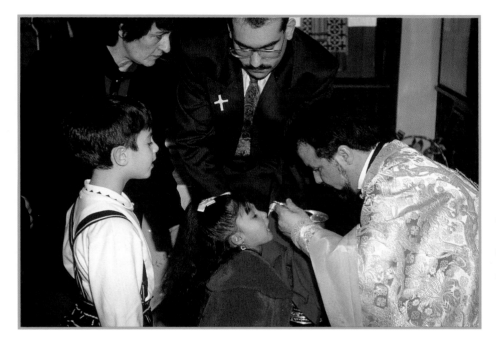

The priest uses a spoon to give communion.

While people are taking communion, the **choir** sings **hymns** and **anthems**. At the end of the liturgy everyone is invited to eat a small piece of bread. It comes from the same loaf as the bread given in communion. This shows that they all belong to the worshipping **community**.

Lent and Easter

Orthodox Christian festivals are celebrated in church. The most important is **Easter**. During Lent, the time before Easter, **worshippers fast**. People choose only a few things to eat and drink. This helps them think more about **God** and less about food.

During the week before Easter Sunday, Christians remember what happened in the last week of **Jesus**'s life. On the Friday evening, the time when Jesus was buried, an **icon** of his body is placed in a carved wooden frame which represents his **tomb**.

Girls decorating the wooden frame.

Easter Sunday

At midnight on Easter Saturday a joyful celebration of Jesus's **resurrection** begins. Some worshippers light their candle from the **priest**'s candle. Then they pass the light to others. Soon the dark church is lit by a blaze of lights. Worshippers greet each other by saying 'Christ is risen', and answering 'He is risen indeed'.

Just after midnight on Easter Sunday morning.

Festivals and ceremonies

Each year twelve other great festivals are celebrated in church. They recall events in the life of **Jesus** and Mary, his mother.

Orthodox worshippers believe their lives are gifts from **God**. From their birth they are on a journey back to God. Each important stage on the way is marked by prayers and worship.

Babies are brought to church to be baptized and **anointed** with oil. **Baptism** is the ceremony that makes babies part of the **Church**.

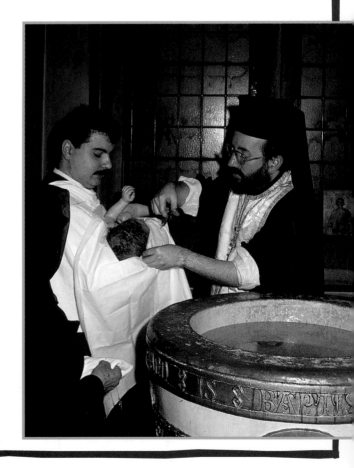

Preparing a baby for baptism.

More steps along life's way

Young people and adults come to tell God they are sorry for wrong things they have done.

At a wedding the **priest** crowns both bride and groom to show they are to be like a king and queen in their own family.

At someone's funeral worshippers ask God to forgive anything that person did wrong in his or her life.

The most important thing that happens in the church is linking the worshippers with God through prayer.

A bride and groom are crowned at their wedding.

Glossary

altar table in the sanctuary used during important parts of the liturgy

altar boy boy or young man who helps the priest during the liturgy

anoint touching the head and other parts of the body with a special oil

anthem song of worship sung by the choir

banner embroidered cloth, hung on a pole and carried in processions

baptism (BAP-tiz-um) ceremony making people part of the Church

Bible (BY-bull) Christian holy book

bishop Church leader in charge of all the churches in a part of a country

bless to pray that God will use people or things to bring joy and happiness

choir (KWIRE) group of singers

Christ name given to Jesus by Christians who believe he is the son of God

Christian (KRIS-tee-AN) someone who follows the religion of Christianity. Christians believe in God, and his son Jesus.

Christmas festival when Christians celebrate Jesus's birth

Church when church has a capital C, it refers to the whole Christian community

communion (kom-YOO-nee-un) eating bread and drinking wine offered to God in the liturgy

community (KOM-yoo-nittee) group of people who share the same beliefs

community centre place where a community meets

cross sign which reminds Christians of Jesus's death on the cross (usually an empty cross to show their belief in Jesus's resurrection)

deacon (dee-kun) man who helps the priest and sings a part of the liturgy

disciple one of Jesus's closest followers

dome special round roof

Easter Christian festival recalling Jesus's death and his resurrection

fasting not eating or drinking certain foods for a time, as a devotion to God

God Christians believe that God made, sees and knows everything

Gospels title of four books in the Bible, 'good news' about Jesus's life and teaching

heaven for Christians, God's home

holy means specially respected because it has to do with God

hymn song sung in church to worship God

icon (EYE-kon) holy picture painted to help people think about God

iconostasis (eye-kono-STA-sis) icon-covered screen which divides the sanctuary from the rest of the church

incense sweet smell made by burning spices

liturgy service of worship which ends with Holy Communion

Jesus Christians believe that Jesus is the son of God

name day day when the saint whose name you were given is remembered

Orthodox Greek word meaning 'right belief' and also 'right worship'. Orthodox Christianity is a kind of Christianity.

Orthodox Church when church begins with a capital C it means the whole Orthodox Christian community

priest man who performs the most important parts of the worship and cares for the lives of worshippers

procession people walking in an orderly line

resurrection (rez-erek-shun) Christian belief that God made Jesus alive again after his burial

saint person who once lived close to God and who is honoured by the Church

sanctuary part of church containing altar and other things used in worship

service meeting in church to worship God

sign of the cross gesture with the right hand, touching forehead, chest and both shoulders, reminding worshippers of Jesus's death on the cross

tomb (TOOM) hollow space cut out of rock to contain a dead body

worship (WUR-ship) show respect and love for God

worshippers people who show respect and love for God

Index